Dedication

I wish to express a debt of gratitude to the men and women who have endured my preaching throughout the years. My thoughts come from the many years I have studied God's Word in order to help them along their spiritual journey. In the best way I can say it, "Thank You for allowing me the privilege of not only being your pastor, but your friend."

I also wish to express tremendous gratitude to my beautiful wife, Jennifer. She has been my most ardent supporter not just in the ministry but throughout our entire marriage. This book is only due to her love all these years.

Last, but certainly not the least, Jesus Christ of Nazareth. May you discover Him in these pages.

All for Christ,
Dr. Raymond Grabert

Coffee With The Preacher:

A Devotional Companion for the Gospel of John

Coffee With
The Preacher:

A Devotional Companion for the Gospel of John

Dr. Raymond Grabert, Jr.

TABLE OF CONTENTS

Introduction

I love coffee, but I love God's Word even more. I have a desire for both in my life and when I can mix the two together, life is good. I have spent a lifetime devoted to both coffee and God's Word. The devotional you hold in your hands is my attempt at blending a good cup of java with God's Word. Grab a great cup of java, your Bible, and your favorite study spot and get started. The devotions are designed to be cup sized but thought provoking. Allow the Holy Spirit to speak to you as you read the Bible passages. Dwell on the importance of each passage and allow Him to stir your heart and mind. Grab your cup of java and walk through John's gospel!

All for Christ,

Dr. Raymond Grabert

Cup 1 - John 1:1-18

I grew up in a Southern Baptist church in South Louisiana. I attended Sunday School from a very early age into adulthood. I loved it when my teacher would ask questions. I paid attention knowing she would ask us what we remembered. I just loved answering her and seeing her kind eyes light up even when we gave wrong answers. Allow me to ask you a question: Do you know why Jesus came? Sure! You may be thinking to yourself. He came to bring us salvation. You would be correct but that is not His only accomplishment. John wants us to recognize His broad impact. We can gain a better perspective when we view Jesus through John 1:18. He came as God incarnate in order for us to understand the nature and character of God the Father. Jesus' mission included showing us the Father's love and the depth of that love. We tend to limit our understanding of the gospel message when we only think the stories of Jesus point just to the cross. Take your time and consider what the gospel is revealing about God the Father and His character and interaction with humanity.

Father, help me to see Jesus afresh as I start my journey through John's gospel writing. Open my eyes to see Jesus as the Son of God, God incarnate. May my heart experience excitement and joy as I walk through the stories which all point to who Jesus is as Your Son, my Savior.

Amen

Notes to Remember

Cup 2 - John 1:6-9, 19-28

What is your purpose in living? Our purpose for living can change from year to year. I remember my purpose as a kid: get through the school year so I can enjoy my summer break. Of course, a second purpose was to make good grades so Mom and Dad would be happy with me and I would progress to the next grade! Certainly my purpose for living changed when I became an adult. Purpose drives our actions, words, and attitudes. Who we are striving to become, in part, is based on our purpose(s) in life. What guides your actions daily? John the Baptist knew his purpose. His purpose led him to be able to testify about Jesus with clarity. Your actions will point to or away from Jesus. The challenge you face, as a believer in Jesus, is to live your life in a way that others around you can see the characteristics of God. We are in a salvation relationship with God the Father, therefore the change that He has made in us is to be lived out. The process of being saved is a major life event. Our very nature is changed by God the Holy Spirit.

Heavenly Father, may my purpose for living be grounded in You. May my life be lived in such a way that You are given glory by my words, actions, thoughts, and attitudes. Holy Spirit, you are free to change me into the person that is like Jesus my Savior.

Amen

Notes to Remember

Cup 3 - John 1:29-33

"It's a boy!" was my cry when both my sons were born. I was so excited that I called everyone I knew. I even brought my firstborn to see my home church pastor at work. I was so excited to have experienced the birth of my son that I could not wait to tell people of the new life that had entered the world. Have you shared good news like this? You get a raise at work! A substantial raise at that! What did you do? Did you phone home and share that excitement with those you love? You would share that with your family and friends. Jesus has done something for us which is way beyond a substantial raise. The question comes to us: "What do you tell people about Jesus?" John the Baptist clearly articulated what he knew about Jesus. He plainly spoke to his disciples the truth of Jesus. He pointed out that Jesus was the Messiah. He left nothing in question, Jesus was the greater one. You have the responsibility to clearly articulate who Jesus is to your loved ones, friends. They need to understand why you value Jesus in your life the way you do. The only way they will gain that understanding is if you share with them as John the Baptist did with his disciples. Share specifics do not skimp on the details!

Jesus, help me to share what you have done for me with others who are in my life. Renew within me the joy I first had when You saved me. Help me articulate with others who You are to me and how You can do the same for them. Use me as You used John the Baptist!
Amen

Notes to Remember

Cup 4 - John 1:35-42

Do you remember the last request you made of someone? It may have been just moments ago. When you made your request, it was based on the expectation of receiving. One of my favorite foods is a shrimp casserole my wife bakes. I love making that request of her. More importantly, she loves me and cooks it for me. I have come to expect that wonderful dish when I request it. John the Baptist's declaration of the identity of Jesus as the Lamb of God caused two of his disciples to follow Jesus. They had an expectation of Jesus based on John's words. The two disciples of John the Baptist followed at a distance planning to speak with Jesus. He, however, before they could speak turned around and addressed them. He asked them a question which focused them on their expectations. When you come to Jesus, He will ask you the same question. Your purpose of coming to Jesus initially can be born of curiosity. However, you soon discover that Jesus calls you to examine His invitation. A relationship with Him is no small life event. He wants to transform your life, and this takes a willingness on your part to deal with the gospel message with honesty and openness. Your willingness to stop and consider what you really want from Jesus is the beginning of a wonderful journey to a relationship with our heavenly Father.

Father, help me answer the all-important question, "What do I expect of You?" Give me wisdom and insight to understand what I desire. Help me be honest with myself and with You.

Amen

Notes to Remember

Cup 5 - John 1:48-51

You are in a room filled with people and you see the person who will end up being your spouse. Did you already know everything about that individual? Of course not. You had to meet them first and then spend time getting to know them. Love for that person had to grow from infancy to maturity. When I met Jennifer, I knew nothing except she was a beautiful woman. We could not speak for about an hour after meeting because we were in a revival service! Talk about a good start! Thankfully, she agreed to a first date at Pizza Hut and the rest is history. The early disciples had to get to know Jesus. They had to start at the beginning in their relationship with this new rabbi. Time had to be given, early conversations may have lasted long into the night as Jesus engaged them in questions and answers. Your relationship with Jesus is the same. Your understanding of Jesus starts in infancy very much like all other relationships. Therefore, you must spend time getting to know Him. The challenge you face is to be open to Jesus. Your faith relationship grows as you open yourself to Jesus and allow Him to shape you into a godly person. You are no different than the early disciples, you must get to know Jesus as they did.

Jesus, help me to get to know more of You. Help my knowledge of You increase and may I grow as your disciple as time passes.

Amen

Notes to Remember

Cup 6 - John 2:1-12

No man is an island is a popular and well-known phrase. It certainly rings true for me. I am a social creature. Sometimes I need to be with people. While solitary study is good, there are times I need teh social interaction of being with others. God created us to be social beings. We are never to live isolated from others. Even Jesus, though He was God, did not withdraw from people. His first miracle/sign was performed in the presence of a large group of people. The turning of the water into wine occurred at a wedding which was a social event. We discover that Jesus could live among humanity and not give in to sin. Our challenge is to live in social settings with Jesus at the fore front of our words, attitudes, and actions. People can see Jesus as we are interacting with others. We live for Jesus. Others see we are committed to Him and the Holy Spirit is given an opportunity to work in their lives. Do not withdraw from social settings, they are opportunities for Jesus to be injected into the lives of those we meet.

Father, help me to live for You in the midst of the crowds in my life. May You be able to reach those around me with the gospel of Jesus Christ of Nazareth. Give me the ability to live and share!
Amen

Notes to Remember

Cup 7 - John 2:13-25

What are you passionate about? I love coffee. I was raised drinking the golden elixir! Some of my earliest memories are climbing into bed with mom and dad and having a sip of coffee with them. Since then, coffee has been a staple in my life. At one point, I had over a dozen glass vacuum coffee makers in my office. Coffee is a passion for me. Actions, words, and attitudes all stem from our passions. Our passion for Jesus Christ should surface in obvious actions. We reveal what we believe about Jesus through our actions. The thoughts and passions of our hearts translate into observable actions. Our choice of words in all circumstances show our passions. Actions we take, which are born in the passions of the heart will either demonstrate a love or hate for Jesus. We follow the example of Jesus as He cleansed the Temple. He was
passionate about His Father's house. When others see our actions, perceive our attitudes, and hear our words, what would they say we are
passionate about? Would they be able to say we are a follower of Jesus Christ? What would they say?

Father, help me to not only find my passion for You, but to so live my life by that passion. May my passion for Your righteousness and holiness be revealed by how I live my life and bring glory to Your holy name.

Amen

Notes to Remember

Cup 8 - John 3:1-21

Ever hear something that truly amazed you? Maybe it was a new discovery. Could have been a new product that was just released. Nicodemus learned from Jesus that a restart in life was possible. Jesus and Nicodemus were having a discussion. Jesus made a remarkable statement that was remarkable in the ears of Nicodemus. Was that possible? The impossible made possible! Ever make a mistake that made you wish for a second chance? The mistake of a bad choice. The unwise partnership. The sinful habits and actions which hurt us and others. These mistakes can make us wish for a restart in life. The problem with moving past mistakes of the past is belief that a restart is impossible. Jesus revealed to Nicodemus that a restart is available in Him. How is this possible? Jesus Christ points to Himself as the answer. When we place our trust in Him, He gives us a restart in life. When we come to Jesus, He puts our lives in order. Past mistakes do bring us consequences; however, Jesus gives us the ability to start again, and we do not have to live crippled lives under the shadow of a sinful past.

Father, I need a restart in my life. Thank you that You are willing to give me a new beginning. Help me to deal with my sinful past and in the power of Jesus Christ of Nazareth. May my actions in the future be grounded in and through You, my God!
Amen

Notes to Remember

Cup 9 - John 3:22-36

What is your motto? If you summed up your passions and cares into a simple phrase, what would it be? John the Baptist would answer that question, "He must take center stage as I exit stage left!" John knew his role very well. He understood he was to prepare the way for Jesus to take the spotlight. Though his disciples wrestled with that motto, John the Baptist had it down in his heart and mind. How would you summarize your life's direction and goals? Several years ago, I was wrestling with formulating a motto for myself. I simply looked at my life and asked God to help me express my desire in life. "All For Christ!" came to mind. So much so that I now sign any correspondence with that by-line. The motto not only describes where I have been, but what I want to be today. I want Jesus glorified by my life, nothing left out. Your life has a motto whether you can express it right now or not. The things you give attention to and spend money on all point to a motto you live by.

Father, help me to live for You as John the Baptist. May my life be focused totally on You. Help me to live by a motto that expresses my dependence upon You.

Amen

Notes to Remember

Cup 10 - John 4:1-28

Where are you seeking help with life's problems? The woman at the well had problems which needed a solution. Her solution was to go to the well at less busy times to avoid meeting people. John shares with us that she came to the well this one day when Jesus was there. A wonderful conversation ensued which not only challenged her but pointed her to the solution for her life's problems. The conversation was intense, but she came to the realization that she had just found her solution. As a result, she left her water pot behind as she ran to tell others about her conversation. This water pot was the symbol of her self-effort at trying to fix her life. The water pot had been ineffective so, she left it!

When I needed financial assistance with tuition, I went to the Financial Aid office for help. Their expertise in the field of finances helped me fund my education. I went to the right place for the need I had. When I faced interpersonal problems, I did not go back to the financial aid counselor. They did not have the solutions for those problems. Where do you go for solutions to your life's problems? If you are like the woman at the well, you are trying to solve your problems your way only to meet with frustration after frustration. The challenge for us is to abandon our "water pot" for trust in Jesus Christ. Jesus wishes to be our solution for issues which confront us daily. His presence in our lives replace our self-efforts.

Father, help me to recognize You are my help in troubled times! May I have wisdom to see Your perfect will and embrace it.

Amen

Notes to Remember

Cup 11 - John 4:29-45

Our last cup devotional continues in this cup as we consider where are our eyes? The woman at the well had eyes focused on the water pot when she approached the well. She leaves as the disciples arrive back from town. They are shocked to discover He had been talking to her. Their focus is on social norms but, behind them a field is ready for harvest. They needed simply to turn around and see! Where are your eyes? What are you seeing when you drive down the road? What are you seeing when you shop at Wal-Mart? What are you seeing when you get fuel for your car? We tend to be short-sighted. We can go through the motions and never see the people around us. We may "see" them but not "SEE" them. We are busy looking at our needs and are blinded to others around us. Others who are carrying burdens like us. Others who are hurting like us. Others who desire a restart in life. What is the difference? Jesus! The disciples needed Jesus to redirect their eyes. Imagine as they turn around and see a group of people being led by the woman who was just talking with Jesus at the front leading the way. Jesus' words burning in their hearts as He speaks of truly looking and "seeing" people, not just "seeing" them.

Jesus, may I see others around me as You see them. Give me strength to develop an outward focus instead of an inward, selfish focus of living.

Amen

Notes to Remember

Cup 12 - John 4:46-54

I remember times in college when I did not know how I was going to pay for tuition. I knew God had called me to attend and promised He would provide. However, I could not see how. My role was not to know all the details. I was simply to trust and believe God would supply, and that He did! My wife and I made it through. The Royal official approaches Jesus with a need. His need was great! His son was sick back home, and he knew from testimony that Jesus could heal. He asked Jesus for help. To his initial dismay, Jesus told him to return home, and the boy would be healed. His faith in Jesus was challenged at that very moment. Could Jesus really heal from a distance? The official trusted Jesus and headed home. The next day as he traveled, news came that his son was healed at the very hour the official believed Jesus. Jesus calls us to believe even when we cannot clearly see an earthly solution. We demand to see before we can trust. However, faith is not faith if we must have concrete proof before we place our trust in Him. Salvation is guaranteed to those who can move beyond the need for evidence and simply believe!

Father, may I learn the lesson of the official and believe without having to "SEE." May I lean into You with dependence grounded in faith without having to have proof that You will do what You promise.

Amen

Notes to Remember

Cup 13 - John 5:1-16

I enjoy being a shade tree mechanic. I have learned that some diagnostic questions do not seem to make sense until one realizes the questions lead to a real solution. This is what we encounter in this passage. The place is full of sick people longing to be healed. Jesus comes into the place and asks a crippled man if he really wanted healing! My mind cries out, "What?" The cripple man should have wanted healing because he was in the place of healing! The crippled man had to face Jesus' question as we still do today. Do we really want to be made well? Having Jesus bring healing involves us leaving a life we may be accustomed to living, even enjoying. The crippled man may have liked begging and being helped around from place to place. No real responsibility placed upon him, since he was crippled. Before coming to know sinfulness from God's Word, we may enjoy our sinning. Living how we want with no accountability, or so we think. Jesus desires us to encounter Him to be forgiven and healed. However, let us be clear on what that means. We will be fundamentally changed. Our ways are now to be given over to the glory of God the Father. Our actions and attitudes are to be brought under the control of the Holy Spirit. Our lives change from being selfish to being God-centric. Do you really want to be made well?

Jesus, may my heart's desire be for genuine healing and spiritual well-being. May my tendency to remain in my sinful state be replaced with a burning desire to allow You to bring healing only You can provide.

Amen

Notes to Remember

Cup 14 - John 5:17-47

A skill I have had to learn is the ability to outline. I started to learn outlining in an English class. Knowing the parts of a sentence led to a greater understanding of English. Jesus outlines for us in this passage the process of salvation. Do you know the process of salvation? For one to be saved, one must hear the "Good News." Salvation begins when one hears and understands the message of the gospel. We certainly have a huge problem which is sin. Start with Genesis and discover how Adam brought sin into the human equation. Since Adam, sin has been passed down from generation to generation. Everyone is a sinner. A person who dies in their sin goes to Hell which is the judgment of God upon sin. The "Good News" is Jesus came and paid the price for our sin on the cross. His sacrifice paid our sin debt. This is the basics of the "Gospel." Once the message of the Gospel is understood, one must decide whether to place one's faith and trust in Jesus Christ or to reject and turn away from God. God extends an invitation. We must decide what to do with that invitation. By placing our faith and trust in Jesus Christ, we are granted salvation. Jesus wants us to clearly understand that salvation is available to all who believe.

Father, thank You for providing a way of escape for me. Thank You for accepting me when I surrendered my life to You. Take me and use me for Your kingdom. Use me to share with others what I have experienced.

Amen

Notes to Remember

Cup 15 - John 6:1-15

Why are you a disciple of Jesus Christ? The feeding of the 5,000 raises this interesting question of motives. I remember the first time I questioned my motives for going to worship. I was around 18 years of age. I woke up one Sunday morning with a sense of needing to decide something. After having breakfast, the weight of what I woke up to hit me. What was I going to do that day? In that moment in time, a plethora of options surfaced in my heart. I could go out and spend that day for myself or I could decide to go to worship. My mind ran over reasons why to worship God and why I could just spend my time on me. The choice came easily, Jesus had saved me. I chose to worship Yahweh! I remember it as if it were yesterday. The people who were fed by Jesus that day experienced a wonderful miracle/sign. They recognized the situation, an isolated place, no food, a lot of people needing to be fed. A hush falls on the crowd as Jesus blesses the little boy's meager lunch. How could such a small amount feed this great crowd? Whispers turn into shouts, "Jesus is feeding us!" Many in that crowd decided to follow Jesus simply because He fed them. They missed the point that He was God incarnate. They missed the point that Jesus wanted to provide more than their physical needs. They simply wanted a "Manna Messiah!" Why do you follow Jesus Christ?

Jesus, I make You my heart's desire, not just on Sundays, but every day of the week I live. You have given your life so I may live. I dedicate my life to living and worshiping You all the days of my life.

Amen

Notes to Remember

Cup 16 - John 6:16-21

Supplemental texts: Matthew 14:33; Mark 6:51
I spent a lot of time fishing with my father. I know the water. I fell into the water a few times and discovered I had to swim or risk drowning. Though I knew how to swim, the fear of drowning was always there. The risk of drowning creates fear in us, even when we know how to swim. The disciples knew water too! They understood the relationship we share with water. We understand their fear when storms arises, and the boat fills with water. What will happen? Doubt may have crossed their minds, but then a figure appears on the surface of the water. Their fear of the water gave way to fear of another sort. Here is a person walking on the water! Quickly they hear Jesus call out to them. It is their friend and teacher drawing near to the boat. The disciples went from fear to relief in a moment. As Jesus was welcomed into the boat, three actions took place in their lives which we also experience too. First, they were willing to accept Jesus into the boat. The idea to the word "willing" is to purpose, to desire, to prefer. They were willing to accept Jesus into the boat. Secondly, they worshiped Jesus. Jesus walking on the water revealed Him as the Son of God. They responded as only creation can, worship! Thirdly, they embraced a holy awe. The disciples were in awe and were astounded by what they had witnessed. No one had ever walked on water before. Jesus as Creator God had command over creation.

Lord Jesus, may I allow You into my life even in the times of great fear. I give You, me! Let's commune together as I experience Your peace amid life's storms.

Amen

Notes to Remember

Cup 17 - John 6:22-29

Motives are everything. Why we do what we do matters. When I surrendered to the ministry, my motives were questioned by godly men who understood that motives matter. They posed several serious questions to me about my sense of call to the ministry before they were willing to license me and then later ordain me to the Gospel Ministry. I learned that motives matter. Jesus had been on the eastern side of the Sea of Galilee feeding the 5,000. The next morning without a boat (He walked across!), He was found on the western shore. The people questioned Him about it. Responding to their questions, Jesus pointed out their motives for seeking His presence. Why we come to Jesus matters as much as the effort we put into our search. Jesus noted the people were only interested in being fed as they had experienced on the opposite side of the Sea of Galilee. Why we come to Jesus matters a great deal. Jesus taught them and now us that God wants us to come to Him believing in Him as the Son of God, God incarnate! We are to come to Him believing. Motives matter.

Father, I lay my motives open and bare before Your holy and righteous presence. Help me to see wrong motives I have for seeking Your face and grant me wisdom and help to correct them. May I forever seek You the way You desire for me to seek You.

Amen

Notes to Remember

Cup 18 - John 6:30-50

John has been very careful to craft his gospel that we would have a solid idea that Jesus is the Son of God. Growing up in a Christian home, my mother and Sunday School teachers helped me understand not only who Jesus was, but what He came to do. Jesus beautifully reveals He is the long-awaited Messiah who provides. Using the image of bread in the Old Testament, Jesus declares He is the Bread of Life. As the image of bread denotes provision in the Old Testament, He provides what humanity needs to live and thrive. He was not just regular bread. The Jew's ancestors ate the manna in the wilderness but eventually died. For anyone who comes to Jesus the Messiah, death is abolished in His work on the cross. Followers of Jesus live forever. Death no longer has a hold on them. Jesus accepts anyone who humbly comes to Him. The will and plan of God the Father is for the welfare of His creation. God desires for all of us to have an abundant life. That life is found solely in and through Jesus Christ of Nazareth. One must believe that Jesus is God incarnate to find life. The passage is a beautiful reminder that God invites us to salvation.

Father, May I know You as the bread of life, and my heart be inclined toward You. May I come to know who You are and why You came. May You be the bread of life that brings me salvation.

Amen

Notes to Remember

Cup 19 - John 6:51-71

Invitations are fun to receive. They announce such events as birthday parties, anniversary celebrations, or general gatherings. I get excited when I receive due to the coming celebration. After reading the invitation, I must respond. Invitations usually come with four little letters: RSVP. These letters are a request for you to inform the sender of your ability or inability to attend the gathering. Jesus has issued all men and women an important invitation. The content of the invitation is clear, and Jesus makes it clear as He has revealed Himself as the "Bread of Life." God desires for us to find forgiveness of our sins and that forgiveness comes through Jesus Christ of Nazareth. We are called upon, therefore, to make a choice. Will we accept Jesus as Messiah or reject Him? Can we accept our sinful status? Can we suppress the sinful urges of pride and embrace humility? When we can humble ourselves and accept our condition then we can respond favorably to Jesus' invitation to salvation. We can be like Peter. When pressed, Peter looked at Jesus and declared that he preferred to be with Jesus. He understood Jesus had life and was willing to share that life with him and all who accepted the invitation.

Jesus, I accept Your invitation to eternal life. Help me to always live with a sense of humility before You. May I remember who I am, who You are, and live accordingly. Thank You for issuing me Your invitation and moving in my life.

Amen

Notes to Remember

Cup 20 - John 7:1-36

Growing up I was always taught God is love. He is too! "Jesus loves me this I know...." is a song we are taught as children. We learn of different characterizations of Jesus as we grow, but one characteristic we are not always taught is that Jesus was passionate. I do not ever remember hearing a pastor say that Jesus was a passionate individual. I wonder why that is? Do we relegate the character of passionate to the sensual alone? I hope not; let me explain. Jesus was passionate about doing the will of God the Father. He was consumed by staying true to the plan and purpose of God the Father for His, Jesus the Son of God's, life. He takes a low-key approach to the Festival of Shelters to prevent causing undue disruption by His presence. He was passionate for truth. His debating with the religious leader is evidence of His love for truth. He challenges them to judge according to righteous not outward religious standards. Jesus was a passionate Messiah and because of His passion He intentionally moved toward the cross where He would give His life for you and me. Let's add "passionate" to our descriptors of Jesus so we can more fully appreciate His life-giving gift of salvation.

Jesus, help me to understand You more fully. Help me to have the same kind of passion for the will of God to be accomplished in me by embracing Your truth. May I be passionate and give my life in serving You!

Amen

Notes to Remember

Cup 21 - John 7:37-52

Ever just listen to politicians? During election periods, promises pour out of the mouths of those who are vying for your vote. They will promise the moon but once elected, those promises seem to evaporate into thin air. Want to learn how to keep promises? Promise something to your child! As a father of two sons, they helped me learn how to promise and keep that promise. Many times, I made a rash promise to placate them for some issue only to have my words brought back to memory when I had to pay up. Jesus makes a remarkable promise to us. He promised that if we surrendered to Him, He would give us life from deep within. Certainly, Jesus was referring to salvation. He used the imagery of water to help us understand the eternal life He brings to those who take Him at His word. He promised that anyone who believed in Him, life would be bestowed upon that person and that it would be a water that would always satisfy. What a promise! The best part is that we do not have to worry about whether He will deliver or not. Jesus sealed His promise with His blood on Calvary. He set forever the promise of eternal life for all who come to Him and believe.

Jesus, thank You that when You promise something You never go back on Your word. Thank You for securing salvation for me and for the living water flowing in my life because of Your promise!

Amen

Notes to Remember

Cup 22 - John 8:1-11

The stories in John's gospel are so "human." We can see ourselves in them. This cup's story is all too real. I can see myself in the place of the woman because I have, and still do, make mistakes. I tend to err and hurt myself and others in the process. Then again, I can see myself in the place of the legalistic Pharisees. I can easily slip into a mean-spirited accuser of others pointing out their faults and failures. This is why I consider these stories so "human." Regardless of the characters, I identify with them. One character in the stories I strive to identify with but always come up short-Jesus! He is remarkable in His reaction to the whole situation. John 3:17 comes flooding back to my mind when I read this story. Jesus did not come to judge or condemn us. We already stand condemned in our sinfulness. He came to deliver us from our bondage to sin. The woman is us in our sinfulness. No escape possible. No amount of explaining suffices. We are all guilty of sinning against God, our Creator, our heavenly Father. We are certainly worthy of being given the death sentence. God has every right to mete out the punishment of death. However, Jesus forgives this woman and sets her free! Remember the gospel story is about redemption. Jesus came to earth to set us free from our bondage. Jesus would give His life for ours so He could forgive her and us! Peace enters our lives when we realize Jesus is not about condemnation but restoration.

Jesus thank You for giving me the precious gift of salvation. Thank You for giving Your life so that my life may be lived to the fullest. May I live my life "in You" all my days.

Amen

Notes to Remember

Cup 23 - John 8:12-20

Light is wonderful! Having light during the day is good, but having light in the darkness of night is superb. I consider the developments in the area of the light bulb since I was a child and am amazed. I remember how my grandmother had one light bulb hanging in the middle of her living room. One solitary lightbulb hanging by its wire to give its meager light. She would be impressed by our LED lights which cost just about the same as her little bulb did back in the day but give an incredible amount of light. Until Jesus came as the "Light of the World," the Old Testament prophets were like that solitary light bulb. At the time of their prophecy, their light was appreciated and very much needed by God's people. Jesus the Son of God arrives, and His light superseded the Old Testament prophet's light by leaps and bounds. When He announces He is the "Light of the World," the people stop and take note of what He just said. They, like us, understand the value of light. We need light, especially at night to help us navigate our world in safety. Without light, we cannot move in the dark without hitting what is in our way or worse still, falling off a cliff! The Old Testament prophets testified of one who would come to give us the light of God so we would be able to live in safety. Jesus uses the imagery of light to help us understand: He is God, He gives guidance, and He imparts life. He is the fulfillment of the Old Testament prophecies.

Father, may I live in the light of Jesus Christ of Nazareth. May I allow Your words and commands to guide me to life in Jesus.

Amen

Notes to Remember

Cup 24 - John 8:21-30

Very few of us likes or embraces confrontation. We tend to see confrontation in a negative light. Over the years as a pastor I have learned that confrontation can be beneficial when used in the right manner. Confrontation can help us see truths we do not like to see, especially in ourselves. John's gospel was written to help us understand who Jesus is and why He came to earth. When we genuinely seek to understand, we are confronted within ourselves truths we do not like. If we have a negative view of confrontation, we may withdraw and no reap the benefits of coming to know the truth about Jesus. Take a moment to consider the confrontation that takes place within us when we seek to understand Jesus Christ of Nazareth: We wrestle with what separates us from God the Father, we stand face to face with our truest need, and we realize our spiritual blindness. This confrontation begins with the all-important question which was asked in this Cup's passage, "Who are you?" (Asked by the people of Jesus)

Jesus, reveal to me who You are. Help me accept the confrontation with the truths found in this passage. May I not shy away from the conflict within me. May I learn more of You and embrace the salvation You bring to the humble.

Amen

Notes to Remember

Cup 25 - John 8:30-47

A rock exists in nature that resembles gold. It is called pyrite. The first time I came across this rock, I thought I had found gold! I had seen enough western shows to understand that I was rich! What a letdown when I learned the truth! A person can look like a believer but not be genuine. A person can play the part as an actor would a character on the silver screen and deceive others and themselves. Jesus clearly understood we needed help in ensuring our authenticity. In this cup's passage we recognize that a genuine believer "Continues" following Jesus. A fundamental change takes place, and we commit to living as Jesus instructed us. We also grow in our understanding of Jesus and His Word (Bible). Time is spent in meditation and study of the word of God in both the Old Testament and New Testament. As a result, we grow in our faith. As a result of our change and growth we learn to release. We desire to release more of self and embrace more of Jesus. Our hearts are more inclined to live Christ-like and not selfishly. We can evaluate ourselves with these questions: 1. What do I love/hate? 2. Who do I love/hate. 3. Where does my love/hate lead?

Jesus, help me to honestly ask myself these questions. Give me wisdom and insight into myself. Give me clarity as to my genuineness before You! If I find I am genuine, help me celebrate with joy! If I find I am an actor, help me have the courage to repent and to humble myself and seek Your loving forgiveness right now.

Amen

Notes to Remember

Cup 26 - John 8:48-59

How do you keep calm when someone unfairly attacks you? The tendency is to lash back. However, Jesus gives us a better way to respond. Our text recounts a time when the religious leaders accused Jesus of having a demon. Let's look at how He handled it and learn. Three actions may be noted for us. First, Jesus focused on His mission to glorify God the Father. Our actions need to be driven by the Holy Spirit and not by circumstances. The Holy Spirit will always be with us and will never change like external circumstances. Second, Jesus held to the truth. Jesus did not have to "prove" He was not possessed by a demon. He was grounded and firm in His identity. We can resist the temptation to lash out at people who set themselves against us by remembering who we are in Jesus Christ of Nazareth. Falling back upon who has redefined us allows us to live according to the truth of God in us. Third, Jesus relied on the vindication of God. Certainly, Jesus knew resurrection day would arrive. That day would vindicate everything He had said and done. We can live with the assurance, as we live by God's truth in our lives, we will be vindicated. This vindication may come in our lifetime or when Jesus comes again. Following Jesus' example gives us strength to act like His disciples and not a disciple of the world.

Jesus, may I model my behavior after You and not the world. Give me strength to live so You are glorified through my life regardless of the obstacles I may face.

Amen

Notes to Remember

Cup 27 - John 9

What has been the darkest dark you have experienced? I remember a time when the electricity went out at night. A storm had moved in, and I could not see my hand in front of my face. What a night to remember! I was so glad for the flashlight and candles in the house. Jesus is the "Light of the World." He came so we do not have to live in spiritual darkness. The man born blind moved from a state of physical darkness to light. His encounter with Jesus Christ of Nazareth completely changed his life forever in dramatic fashion. He would never experience life in the same way again. He would see life in a new way. Sight and sound connected for the first time. The term "mother" now took on a new dimension. We too can have a fundamental shift in our lives when we have a similar encounter with Jesus. Darkness describes our spiritual lives under the weight of God's judgment. Jesus comes to us and bestows unto us deliverance from sin and judgment. He does so because of His sacrifice on the cross. His shed blood applied to us delivers us. We experience salvation and are fundamentally changed. So drastic is this change that we never live the same again!

Heavenly Father, thank You for the new life You have given me. Thank You that I can make spiritual connections I have never had before. It is all because of Your presence in my life by the Holy Spirit.

Amen

Notes to Remember

Cup 28 - John 10:1-21

Sounds can be comforting. I can still remember the voice of my mother and father just as clear today as I heard them as a child. While they were living, I enjoyed calling them just to hear their voices. Those voices held such dear love to me. Our relationship with Jesus can be similar. We have the Holy Spirit within us. If we develop our relationship with Him, we discover, embrace, and develop a peace from His presence. We can long to hear from Him daily if we recognize He desire to relate to us. Jesus called Himself the Good Shepherd. Shepherds would gather their flocks. The sheep's relationship is very intimate. When a shepherd arrives at the sheep pen, he call out his sheep from among the others being sheltered. Those sheep would hear the voice of their shepherd and would follow him to the open pastures. He would then lead them as he cared for them. Our relationship with Jesus is similar. Hearing His voice, we are comforted by His presence and provision. We, through our relationship with Jesus, experience comfort through His presence.

Jesus, may our relationship be like that of sheep and shepherd. Let us grow close together so I may experience Your comfort as You care for me.

Amen

Notes to Remember

Cup 29 John 10:22-42

For those who know me, I love coffee. I experience joy in the process of making my coffee. From grinding the beans to being sure the water is not too hot, I love my coffee. I love the smell and the taste! There is one thing that brings me greater joy, my relationship with God through Jesus Christ. Nothing can compare to the relationship I have with God. I accepted Christ as Lord and Savior at an early age and God has always guided me thus far. I also love serving Him by preaching and teaching His Word. Nothing can describe the feeling I have when I am finished preaching and teaching. Joy would be one of the top words I would use if pressed. What brings joy into your life? Make a list of your joys. Is Jesus on your list? In our passage, Jesus lays out three spiritual items we receive when we become His disciples: 1) We know His voice. 2) He grants us salvation. 3) He eternally protects us. These create joy in our hearts when we recognize these are ours if we have been saved. If you need a joy boost in your life, meditate over these and allow joy to rise in your heart!

Jesus, thank You for giving me such wonderful gifts. Help me to understand their significance in my life and may it produce in me a tremendous joy which will drive my service to You.

Amen

Notes to Remember

Cup 30 - John 11:1-16

We all have 24 hours in a day, each day. The question that confronts us: "What are you doing with the time you have been given?" When I have a lot to get done, I must ask myself this question. What will I do with my time? Jesus understood the concept of making the most of the time He had been given for His earthly ministry. When news of Lazarus' sickness arrived, He sought out and acted according to the will of God the Father. He deliberately delayed in traveling to Bethany. When Jesus tells His disciples their group was headed to Lazarus, they noted how the religious leaders were hostile and desired to kill Him. Jesus responds with calm assurance and intentionality. He underscored to His disciples that He had twelve hours to do the work of the Father. Nothing, not even hostile religious leaders, could hinder the work He came to accomplish. Everything was in the hands of the Father. Jesus simply sought to accomplish that work. We have been given our own twelve hours. Our lives are finite. We are born, live, and die. Between the events of birth and death is what we call living or life. The question is will we live our lives for the glory of God the Father? Can we live like Jesus with intentionality? What will our lives accomplish for the Father? Can we direct our actions to benefit the Kingdom of God? We have been given spiritual gifts from God the Holy Spirit. Do we use them for His kingdom or do we spend our gifts selfishly on ourselves?

Father, I commit myself to serving You and Your Kingdom. May my actions bring You glory and honor. My desire is to spend my time on Your purpose in my life so others may see You in me!
Amen

Notes to Remember

Cup 31 - John 11:17-46

One of the greatest experiences as a pastor has been witnessing the salvation of an individual. One man always sticks in my mind. He came down the aisle during the invitation and with uplifted hands started shouting, "Save me! Save me!" Following the service, I shared with him the gospel message again. He prayed that day and was saved. His life following that experience was certainly not perfect, but I could see God at work in his life. Have you witnessed the transforming power of God in this manner? Martha and Mary were challenged in their understanding of what Jesus could do in a person's life. Lazarus was dead but death was not the final state of his life. Jesus requests for the stone sealing Lazarus in the tomb to be removed. Both sisters cannot see past the finality of death, but Jesus challenges them with the phrase, "Didn't I tell you..." When we can see past our limiting beliefs, we can witness God's remarkable transforming power in the lives of others around us. Why does this matter? When we believe Jesus can make a difference in the lives of others around us, we ourselves are built-up in our spiritual lives and are excited to share the gospel. He made a difference in us! Let's give others the same opportunity.

Father, use me to share the Gospel with others around me. May I have the joy of seeing others respond in faith as You work through me. Grant to me courage to speak Your truth and allow You to change lives. May I not get in the way, but be Your mouthpiece.

Amen

Notes to Remember

Cup 32 - John 11: 45-57

Life decisions can create irony. When I was first married, I thought when I lost an argument with my wife I was losing as a person. The reality of the situation was the moment was an opportunity to grow as an individual and as a couple. What I considered a negative was a positive. I have learned differently over time. I have had to learn to lose to win. Coming to Jesus Christ is no different. I ask people, "What would prevent you from accepting Jesus Christ as your Lord and Savior?" Responses vary, but the heart of the matter is not wanting to lose. People facing Jesus will respond in one of two ways: acceptance or rejection. Those whose response is one of rejection involves an irony that goes unnoticed, but it exists. Because the person feels he/she will lose something in the relationship, rejection is their answer. Their choice to reject leads to a life that is headed toward destruction and not life. The religious leaders could not see how Jesus brought life, and the result was a deliberate move to have Jesus killed. Fast-forward 40 years and Jerusalem is destroyed by the Romans, and they lost it all. They were to blame, not Jesus. Salvation is completely opposite of what they think they will lose. If you have not surrendered to Jesus Christ for salvation, what prevents you from doing so right now?

Lord, help me to discover in myself where I reject You and why! Help me to repent from my rejection and turn to accepting You to obtain the life You desire to give me.

Amen

Notes to Remember

Cup 33 - John 12:1-11

Flashlights cannot reach their full potential unless it is dark! I have bought new flashlights over the years. I could not wait to charge the light so I could be amazed at the amount of light it gave. Even though I played with the light during the day, I did not understand its full potential until it was set against the darkness of the night. Mary's act of anointing Jesus' feet is such an act which glows for us to not only revel in, but to mimic. The act of anointing comes at a very dark moment in John's gospel. While many are believing in Jesus, the religious leaders are planning His murder. Terms such as hatred, suspicion, treachery, and coldness are descending into the story like a large thunderstorm on the horizon during mid-day. However, Mary's act shines brightly against this backdrop. Some want Jesus dead, but many others are starting to understand He is the Messiah and welcome Him into their lives and homes. Our lives are a light in a dark world which can be characterized by hatred, suspicion, treachery, and coldness toward God the Father. Our acts of devotion shine brightly now more than ever against society's dark background. Let us not grow weary in our devotion to Jesus Christ of Nazareth. Shine your light!

Father, may I not cower in fear of the darkness of society. Give me the courage to continue being devoted to You. Use me to be a light to my family, friends, co-workers, and anyone else I encounter. May my devotion shine strong in my world!

Amen

Notes to Remember

Cup 34 - John 12:12-19

Object lessons are great to help us remember timeless truths. A single lit match in a dark room dispels the darkness and in my young mind left an impression on how people can impact our lives. A single individual can make a significant impact on my life is one lesson I learned from a single match. When Jesus rode into town on a young donkey, He was giving us an object lesson to help us understand important truths about Himself. He was about to undertake the most important act in human history. Through the object lesson of riding into town, we learn first that He is King. He is God incarnate, our Creator and as such, He is King. Second, He is not a warrior king, He is the King of Peace. His very act of sacrificing Himself on the cross secures our peace with God the Father. Our sins forgiven; atonement secured for sinful humanity. He did not come to destroy but to restore! Last of all, He came so we can rejoice in purpose. Sin destroyed our understanding of purpose. Jesus came so we can live in relationship with God the Father and so rejoice in a right relationship. Through a simple act of riding into town on a donkey, we learn timeless truth which shape and change us.

Father may the truths of Your object lesson find its home in my heart. May I see beyond the simple act of You riding into town on a young donkey amid the worship of the people. May I see and embrace the deeper lesson You are teaching me!

Amen

Notes to Remember

Cup 35 - John 12:20-36

The Christian life is a challenge. We are called to become like Jesus in our lives, but we struggle. I know this to be real as I struggle to consistently live like Jesus. Someone may say, "Dr. Raymond, you are a pastor!" Yes I am, but that does not make me a super Christian. If anything, I see the discrepancy between who I am and who God desires me to be. How can I move closer to where God wants me to be? I look to Jesus. Jesus helps us understand how we can be fruitful as He explains the reason for His crucifixion. He uses the analogy of a seed's potential. When a seed is planted into the ground, it undergoes a marvelous transformation. The seed must first die to itself in order for the root and sprout to form. It actually surrenders itself in order to become what it is intended to become. This is what happened when Jesus died on the cross. He surrendered Himself in order to accomplish the will of God the Father, salvation for humanity. We can move closer to God's will for our lives too when we willingly say no to self and yes to God. Hard decision to deny self, but wonderful result when we do.

Father, help me to say no to myself and yes to You. Grant me the wisdom and understanding of Your will and ways so I can make intelligent choices in living my life so You may be honored.

Amen

Notes to Remember

Cup 36 - John 12:37-50

Life is full of choices. One of my first decisions involves the method of coffee brewing. Will I use the pour over or the automatic drip machine? This is just one of hundreds I will make. Life is full of decisions. John wrote his gospel in order for us to make an intelligent decision about Jesus Christ of Nazareth. I have heard people say, "I will deal with Jesus later." I understand about wanting to make an informed decision; however, this issue is so important that it demands we make a decision. The belief that not making a decision is not a yes or no answer. Jesus teaches the importance of choosing. When we resist making a decision about His claims, we are rejecting Him. Any answer but "yes" places us in the "no" category, no third answer exists. Jesus teaches ambivalence is rejecting God the Father. Because Jesus is God the Son, the second person of the Trinity, rejection of the Son is rejection of the Father. We remain in spiritual darkness. Jesus revealed Himself as the "Light of the World" and as such when we reject Him, we remain in darkness. The darkness we live in is the condemnation of the Father on all sin. Only the sacrifice of the Son provides forgiveness and transference into the light. The ultimate result is we miss eternal life.

Jesus, help me make my decision about who You are, why You came, and how I can experience eternal life. Give me understanding where I need it so I may choose You!

Amen

Notes to Remember

Cup 37 - John 13:1-20

Serving others is one of the most Christlike moments in our lives. We set ourselves aside and allow others to be more important. One way I enjoy serving others is during church-wide fellowships. The looks on congregant's faces when I come along with the jug of tea asking if I can refill their glass. They feel special as their need is being met! Jesus washes the feet of the disciples as a demonstration of how they were to serve one another. Peter bawks at Jesus washing his feet because a lowly servant was responsible to perform that task. In his mind, Jesus should not have been performing that task as He was the Messiah. Jesus demonstrated that we are to be willing to divest ourselves of pride and attend to the menial tasks which need to be done. Only in subduing our pride will we be able to minister to others in meaningful ways. We are never to think that we are above scrubbing toilets or mopping the floors when the need arises. Jesus calls us to be attentive and subdue our pride. When we serve, we are indentifying with Jesus in a tangible manner. Our identification with Jesus transforms us from selfish sinners into obedient loving servants.

Jesus, help me to be like You. I surrender my pride. Teach me to serve others as You have served me!

Amen

Notes to Remember

Cup 38 - John 13:21-38

I grew up a New Orleans Saints fan. I remember watching the Saints on television with my dad. We would cheer, yell, and carry on like crazy people when a touchdown was scored. I even let others know I was a fan by wearing a copy of the number "8" jersey. I was proud to let others know I was a fan. Others instantly knew of my devotion! No jersey exists for us to wear so others can see if we are Jesus' followers, or is there? How does an outside world know of our devotion to Jesus? "Love" Love reveals we are disciples of Jesus Christ. As the love of God becomes the standard of interactions with others in the Kingdom, outsiders will recognize you are follower of Jesus. So many different personalities abound that eventually, feelings will be hurt, differences of opinion surface, and toes will be stomped. How those instances are handled by disciples involved reveal their relationship with Jesus. If we treat others in the Kingdom no different than how the world treats their own, then our testimony of Jesus Christ is crippled. When we allow the love of God guides us to relate in love, then others see that God has indeed made a difference in our lives.

Jesus, may Your love for me overflow to others around me. May I treat them as You have treated me. Help me to understand more about Your love so I may in turn extend that love when my feelings get hurt or my toes get stomped. May others see You in me!

Amen

Notes to Remember

Cup 39 - John 14:1-11

Technology can be a blessing. Consider the strides made in recent years with navigation through cell phones. No longer do we need GPS units to tell us when and where to turn. Our phones can direct us where we need to go. Follow the instructions and you will arrive! Note that we must follow its instructions, otherwise, we will not arrive at our intended destination. The disciples were at a loss. Jesus was preparing them for His departure. They desired to know the way in order to follow Him. The questions they asked revealed hearts longing to know the path and not get lost. Jesus, understanding their desires, gives a clear answer to sooth their hearts. We learn from Jesus' response that He is the only way to God the Father. Because Jesus the Son is God the Father, Jesus could equate knowing Him was the equivalence of knowing the Father. Therefore, Jesus can claim that the only way to salvation was through a relationship with Himself. We now know that Jesus is the path to God the Father. The questions is, "Will you follow Jesus?" We gain salvation through a faith relationship with Jesus Christ. We must believe that His statement of being the only way to the Father is correct due to the evidence presented in the Gospel story. Then, we must decide for ourselves whether we will believe and place our faith in Jesus Christ. Follow the evidence of the works and teachings of Jesus and you will discover He leads you to salvation!

Father, reveal Yourself to me through Jesus Christ, Your Son. May I trust His revelation of how to have eternal life. Open my heart to Your message of forgiveness and may I trust Jesus to lead me to You.
Amen

Notes to Remember

Cup 40 - John 14:12-31

We were never meant to be alone. The creation story in the book of Genesis reveals we were created with the need for companionship. God made Adam and then created Eve. Eve was created to be a helper and a companion for Adam. We are no different today. I am a people person. Though I tend to be shy, I still love to be around people. Nothing is more exciting than working on a project with someone else. Jesus understood how He created us. That is why He teaches us about God the Holy Spirit and His relationship with us. Jesus taught about the relationship we would enjoy when God the Holy Spirit would be fulfilled. Because Jesus knew He would not be here physically on earth with His disciples, He provided His presence through the Holy Spirit. Though their relationship with Jesus would change, the relationship with the Holy Spirit would be life to the disciples. The depth of their relationship would deepen as the Holy Spirit brought to them the truth of God through Jesus Christ. They would be in relationship with God the Father, through Jesus Christ's work on the cross, accomplished by the filling of God the Holy Spirit. We today are not alone, even if we are physically alone, Jesus is with us through the indwelling Holy Spirit. We can be assured that we have His presence because of Jesus' promise!

Jesus, grant to me the ability to sense Your presence on a daily basis. Help me to grow in understanding and discerning Your presence.

Amen

Notes to Remember

Cup 41 - John 15:1-8

Jesus' teachings are so vivid and memorable. His use of simple images creates profound lessons which are easy to understand. Having been raised with parents who loved to garden, I easily understand what Jesus is teaching in this passage because I spent a lot of time in the garden helping out. If I am to be fruitful in God's Kingdom, I must maintain a vibrant relationship with Jesus. My life source is Jesus Christ. Productivity is directly related to personal growth as His disciple. The use of the branches and the vine beautifully illustrate the necessity of maintaining our relationship. When mother would prune her tomato plants, the branches she would snip off would quickly wither and die having been removed from the main body of the plant. If we want to be useful to God, we must nurture our relationship with Him. Jesus is our source of life. He is to be depended upon. we must nourish ourselves on His words and teachings so we can produce fruit. The neglect of our relationship with Him leads to selfish living. Our focus is not on God's desires and we are led away from God instead of toward Him. The branches Mother cut from her plants never produced a single tomato. Every branch died there on the ground. Neither can we produce spiritual fruit for God's Kingdom if we lay on the ground separated from Him.

Father, may I grow in my walk with You. Guide me as I give proper attention to our relationship. Help me to be a productive member of Your Kingdom for Your honor and glory.

Amen

Notes to Remember

Cup 42 - John 15:9-25

What is the greatest expression of love? Every year we celebrate love on February 14th. Valentines Day is full of individuals celebrating their love for one another. I am left with a question in my mind, "How can I truly love others?" Jesus gives us the answer to this question and more in our passage. We best love others when we are willing to give our lives for them. We place them first and foremost in our lives. Our words and actions reveal we truly love them for we speak their language not ours. Selfish tendencies are subdued in us in order to give all of what and who we are to see others flourish and abound! One of my professors at Seminary once defined loves as "the giving forth of one's self." I have carried that definition around all these years and they still ring true. That definition is certainly Christ-like in that Jesus states that true love is demonstrated when one person lays his/her life down in the place of another. His love on Calvary certainly reflects definition. The challenge to you and me is for us to model His love on a daily basis to others around us. Unconditional love is one of our greatest challenges because my flesh cries out for selfish fulfillment, and unconditional love means the death of me! Add to this challenge the spiritual element. When I experience the love of Jesus for me, then I not only love others unconditionally, I love God unconditionally too. What a way to demonstrate love!

Jesus, give me wisdom to understand Your love and may I have strength to extend love not only to You, but to others around me in my daily life. I turn from selfish fulfillment to placing others ahead of myself.

Amen

Notes to Remember

Cup 43 - John 15:26-16:15

Who is your best friend? How do we identify our best friend? These questions can be difficult to answer, but before we can answer these questions, we must set some parameters of what constitutes a best friend. Let's start by stating a best friend fits the same characteristics that Jesus gave us of the Holy Spirit. So, let's look at the Holy Spirit and in so doing define a best friend. First of all, the Holy Spirit is Jesus' presence in our lives in the third person of the Trinity. Best friends are present in our lives. This person is not just a casual acquaintance we seldom see but is involved in our lives. Second, the Holy Spirit is comforting to us. The Holy Spirit is defined as one who comes along side of us. Like our best friend! When we need encouragement, they place their arms around us and walk with us. They do not leave when we need them. We can depend upon them. Third, the Holy Spirit speaks truth to us. Our best friend is truthful in all matters. Here, we have a person who will always be honest, and at times, they may be brutally honest to our dismay. A best friend remains a best friend because we know their honesty comes from wanting what is best for us. Now that we have briefly defined a best friend, I have a new question to ask myself, "Is the Holy Spirit my best friend?" Is He yours?

Father, I want You as my best friend. Help me to open myself to You. May I allow You to relate to me as a best friend would. I recognize You only want what is best for me. Help me to be open to Your presence, comfort, and truth.

Amen

Notes to Remember

Cup 44 - John 16:16-33

The cross is only days away and Jesus pours into His disciples as much as they can take in and digest. They will face a coming low in their lives. Jesus will be crucified and buried. Their hope of a Messianic reign will come crashing down. I learned early on that the life of a disciple is full of highs as well as lows. Anyone who has lived any time on this earth knows life throws all kinds of ups and downs our way! Jesus never promised us a life free of troubles and strife. What He did promise was to be with us. He would strengthen us to bear the troubles of this world. How do we receive the strength and joy Jesus brings? Prayer. Simply pray in the name of Jesus Christ. He is our life and connection to God the Father. Note that our asking must be for the will of God the Father to be accomplished. God's purpose for us is that we live in His strength, so we can pray for strength to handle the lows, and I would add, the highs as well. The highs in life can be just as challenging because we tend to not perceive our need or God. Our challenge is to see our need for God daily in our lives and to seek His presence, encouragement, and joy.

Father, grant me Your presence as I walk through the lows of this life. I lean on You for strength to remain faithful to You and Your will for my life. Give me spiritual insight so the highs of my life will not lessen my dependence upon You.

Amen

Notes to Remember

Cup 45 - John 17:1-26

There is something special about having another person praying for you. I remember my mother would constantly tell me she had been praying for me and that she would continue to do so. At the time, I was a young man and did not quite understand the impact prayer can make in one's life. Only until I began preaching did I value her prayers on my behalf. I can still remember walking in on her praying. She was praying for me and a host of others she dearly loved. Did you know Jesus prayed for you while He was here on earth? As He faced giving His life for you, He prayed for you! He prayed intently that we would experience unity with other believers and that we would be protected as we lived our lives out for God's glory and honor. Reread Jesus' prayer, allow the Holy Spirit to speak to your heart as you read Jesus' words. He is praying for our success as disciples in a world that hated Him and now hates us. I understand more about my mother's love for me as I reflect upon what must be countless hours she prayed for me. Similarly, we can understand the depth of Jesus' love for us as we read His conversation with the Father on our behalf.

Jesus, thank You for praying for me. May I understand the great love You have for me. Help me to reflect my appreciation of Your love as I seek to live for You.

Amen

Notes to Remember

Cup 46 - John 18:1-27

Imagine a completely dark room. Light invades the darkness as a match is lit and a candle starts to burn. The light of the candle illuminates the room and we can see. Jesus is the light of the world and as He is arrested, we witness the illumination of the truth of who He is and His courage to carry out the will of God the Father. As the religious leaders question His identity, Jesus answers in an interesting way. He references His works and teachings. Those very miracles and teachings revealed Him to be God the Son the second person of the Trinity. His light was evident for all to witness. I stop here for a moment to consider an important question. Is there enough evidence from my actions, words, and attitudes to reveal Jesus in me? Jesus pointed the religious leaders to His actions for them to make up their own minds about Him. What about me? I claim to be a disciple of Jesus Christ. I want my actions, words, and attitudes to be so close to that of my Savior so others can see that I have sold out to Jesus. What about you? Do you have the same concern as me? If you were to question people in your life, what would they say about you?

Jesus, guide me in living for You. Give me wisdom to know how to live my life so You are made manifest through me. May others around me see You through my life.

Amen

Notes to Remember

Cup 47 - John 18:28-40

Where do we live? Oh, I am not talking about the your physical address of your home. Well, I guess I could expect your answer to include your address. Again, where do you live? A conversation between Jesus and Pontus Pilate took place during Jesus' trial. Pilate is curious to know if Jesus really is a king. No one could claim to be ruler over the people except Rome. Making that claim would bring certain death. Jesus' response is intriguing. He tells Pilate that His Kingdom is not of this world. To prove His point, Jesus notes that His disciples would be taking up arms if His rule was based here on earth. Jesus even chastised Peter for taking up a sword earlier in the garden. Our identification with Jesus shapes our thoughts and actions, therefore, we must consider Jesus' response. If Jesus' kingdom was of this earth, my actions could easily take the shape of the world. I could speak like the rest of the world. I could think like the rest of the world. I could blend in with the world and not stand apart. The realization, however, is Jesus' kingdom is not of this world, therefore, I must speak and act as Jesus desires me to speak and act. My world must be defined and guided by Jesus Christ of Nazareth. I am to stand apart from the world in which I live. They need to see Jesus in me because Jesus' kingdom is not of this world.

Jesus, Your kingdom is not of this world, may I embrace life in Your kingdom and not life in the kingdoms of this world. May others see You in me.

Amen

Notes to Remember

Cup 48 - John 19:1-24

The trial of Jesus before Pilate presents a very intense scene. As I reflect on the moment, I close my eyes and a plethora of sounds and sights fill my mind. I can hear the cursing of the religious leaders, the questioning voice of Pilate, and the cries of the people who are shocked at seeing Jesus being beaten and abused. In the midst of all of these images and sounds stands, Jesus. The image I bear is not a victim of circumstances, but one of meekness. Meekness is not one being weak and a victim of life. The true definition of meekness is strength under complete control. John has beautifully demonstrated that Jesus is the Son of God. At a moment's notice, Jesus could wipe out creation and start over. He does not have to be treated this way by His creation! I say Jesus is the epitome of meekness at this very moment. We see God incarnate with the ability to deliver Himself from this awful death submit to the ultimate will of God the Father. Jesus is the ultimate definition of meekness. Do I live with this kind of meekness? As a disciple of Jesus Christ, can I demonstrate His kind of meekness? Instead of lashing out at others, even when deserved, can I choose to respond with reserve, grace, and mercy? Meekness is to be a part of our lives as a disciple of Jesus. Will you choose meekness?

Jesus, I choose to be like You. Give me wisdom to understand meekness. Grant to me the strength to incorporate meekness into my life. May I respond with meekness in my relationships with others.

Amen

Notes to Remember

Cup 49 - John 19:25-37

Let's consider our greatest accomplishments. If I were to ask you to give me your greatest accomplishment, how would you answer? My answer to that question would be to finish well. I want my life to end in a manner where Jesus gets glory and honor by how I have lived and related to others. Jesus finished well. Even hanging on the cross, He finished the work God the Father gave Him to accomplish. Reflecting on His final words we recognize that He took care of His family. He ensured that Mary (His mother) would be taken care of by John. She was important to Him. Then, He made sure to fulfill all of the Scripture about Himself. John connects the dots for us in that Jesus' declaration of thirst is in fulfillment of Old Testament Scripture. Jesus desired to give us every chance to observe He was the Messiah, God incarnate! Lastly, Jesus completed God the Father's plan of salvation. When He declares the end, the work of securing salvation for humanity was complete. Nothing else needed to be done. Jesus finished well! Reading how Jesus finished well challenges me to do the same. My answer to our beginning question certainly has changed over the years. The younger me would have answered that question a bit differently. Now that I have aged a bit, I see clearer and realize that finishing well is desired and takes me through this life and into the presence of Jesus. Nothing else matters!

Father, give me the strength to finish well. I set my heart on You. Grant to me your wisdom and insights to make wise choices so I may be like my Savior, Jesus Christ, and finish well.

Amen

Notes to Remember

Cup 50 - John 19:38-20:18

The gospel story moves from hopelessness to hopefulness. Jesus has been buried for three days. Hopelessness grips the hearts and minds of the disciples. Their world has crashed, nothing can change the fact that Jesus died. Three days in darkness, then the light! On the first day of the week, news breaks out that Jesus has risen from the dead! What a message. How can one really take that kind of news in? Many witnessed His crucifixion. They saw the soldier thrust a spear into His side. Jesus was dead. So this news coming from Mary Magdalene? Is Jesus alive? Soon they too would see, hear and touch Jesus for themselves. Hope sprung eternal when in their darkest moments, Jesus arrived bringing hope. Hopelessness could not overcome the presence of Jesus Christ. Since that time, the salvation Jesus secured for us has continued to dispel the hopelessness that grips men and women who are in their sin. Remember that the word "gospel" means good news! The good news is that when we repent of our sin and place our faith and trust in Jesus Christ, God saves us! We are indwelt by God the Holy Spirit and hope springs to life in us. We experience new birth in Jesus Christ, not because of who we are but because Jesus is the Messiah, the Son of God!

Jesus, I come asking and desiring the hope that only You can bring into my life. May the "Good News" of salvation spring to life as I repent of my sins and place my trust in You.

Amen

Notes to Remember

Cup 51 - John 20:19-30

John's purpose in writing his gospel is that we today might believe. Someone may say, "I am struggling to believe. Will God forgive me if I am struggling?" Thomas was one of the original twelve disciples. He had witnessed Jesus' miracles. He had heard Jesus' teachings. Thomas may have even had one-on-ones with Jesus. When the news of Jesus' resurrection reached his ears, he struggled to believe. He doubted the report of the resurrection. He declared that he had to personally encounter Jesus in order to believe. Many today are too hard on Thomas. I believe Thomas really typifies many today who hear the gospel story and struggle to put all of the pieces together. God allows us to struggle with identifying and accepting Jesus as the Messiah. However, a word of warning must be given at this juncture. Just because we struggle to understand, the gospel does not alleviate us of the responsibility of making Jesus our Lord and Master. Jesus is God the Son, the second person of the Trinity. God inspired John to write his gospel so we might come to know Jesus and the love He poured out on us. Though we may not be able to reach out and touch the scars in Jesus' hands, we still can experience the life change those scars represent. When we believe by faith, Jesus brings us a change of heart and the feeling of being set free from the chains of sin and death are just as real as those experienced by the first disciples.

Jesus, help me understand; I am struggling. I surrender my struggles over to You. Give me wisdom and insight so I too may have new life.
Amen

Notes to Remember

Cup 52 - John 21:1-25

Have you ever failed in keeping a promise? You boasted you would! The feelings of failing can be overwhelming. This is how Peter felt. Thomas represents when we doubt, Peter represents when we fail. Peter boasted to never abandon Jesus. Jesus' prediction of Peter's threefold failures came true. Many disciples start starry eyed, full of energy and enthusiasm for Jesus. Along the way we experience failure. We fall victim to temptation and Satan comes along poking us in the side with, "God will not forgive that!" We fall for that lie and slide further away from God's presence as we believe we will never be restored. Peter's story presents to us a truth we all need to hear. God is willing to forgive us when we sin after receiving salvation. Three times Peter failed Jesus and three times Jesus led Peter through restoration. Jesus completely restores us when we are willing to be humble and honest before Him. Jesus does not only want to grant us salvation, He wants us to experience a relationship with Him that is vibrant and abundant. Jesus died on the cross so that our relationship with Him radically changes us for the duration of our lives. You may be thinking as you are reading that you have blown it. You question if God is willing to forgive you. Peter's experience tells you the exciting truth that when we repent, Jesus restores us and sets us back on a disciple's path.

Jesus, I know I have sinned. I have fallen for temptation and I am sorry. Please forgive me and give me strength to continue my journey as Your disciple.

Amen

Notes to Remember

Closing Remarks

Thank you for allowing me the privilege of sharing my thoughts on John's wonderful good news of Jesus Christ. My prayer in writing this devotional is for you to come face to face with Jesus Christ of Nazareth. Your encounter would not be from my feeble remarks but through the wonderful, inspired Word of God: the Gospel of John. It is God's story of redemption for all of humanity. So, as you have journeyed through Jesus' story, may God bless you and may you experience His grace and mercy.

All For Christ,

Dr. Raymond Grabert

Author Bio

Dr. Raymond Grabert has been a pastor for 30 years. Currently, he serves as pastor of Big Ridge Baptist Church, D'Iberville, MS. His native state is Louisiana where he met and married his wife of 35 years. Educated at New Orleans Baptist Theological Seminary, he holds the B.G.S, M.DIV., and D.MIN. Degrees.